MUNICH

MUNICH

THE TRUE STORY OF THE ISRAELI RESPONSE
TO THE 1972 MUNICH OLYMPIC MASSACRE
AND THE DEVELOPMENT OF INDEPENDENT
COVERT ACTION TEAMS

ALEXANDER B. CALAHAN

The cover of this book depicts the Seal of The Institute for Intelligence and Special Operations:
"Where no stratagem is, the people fall; but in the multitude of counsellors there is salvation."(Proverbs 11:14)

This book is based on the thesis submitted to the Faculty of the Marine Corps Command and Staff College in partial fulfillment of the requirements for the degree of
Master of Military Studies April 1995
The views in this paper are those of the author and do not reflect the official policy or position of the Department of Defense or the U.S. Government
THIS BOOK IS BASED ON AN OFFICIAL DOCUMENT OF THE MARINE CORPS COMMAND AND STAFF COLLEGE THE OPINIONS AND CONCLUSIONS EXPRESSED HEREIN ARE THOSE OF THE INDIVIDUAL STUDENT AUTHOR AND DO NOT NECESSARILY REPRESENT THE VIEWS OF EITHER THE MARINE CORPS COMMAND AND STAFF COLLEGE OR ANY OTHER GOVERNMENTAL AGENCY.

Alexander B. Calahan
Munich
ISBN-10 1453611231
ISBN-13 9781453611234

Contents

EXECUTIVE SUMMARY

Title: Countering Terrorism: The Israeli Response to the 1972 Munich Olympic Massacre and the Development of Independent Covert Action Teams.

Author: Alexander B. Calahan

Thesis: The purpose of this study is to examine the methodology of the covert action teams authorized by Prime Minister Golda Meir to find and assassinate those individuals responsible for the attack on the Israeli athletes at the Munich Olympic games in September 1972. Specifically, the study addresses whether the operational and tactical methods utilized in this counterterrorist effort were successful relative to the original operational objectives.

Background: In 1972, the Israeli Mossad initiated one of the most ambitious covert counterterrorist campaigns in history. Golda Meir and the Israeli cabinet's top secret 'Committee-X' devised a campaign in retaliation for the massacre of eleven Israeli's during the Munich Olympic games. Meir tasked the committee with devising an appropriate response to the Munich massacre. The panel concluded that the most effective response was to authorize the assassination of any Black September terrorists involved in the Munich incident. The Mossad assumed the responsibility for implementing the panel's directive. To accomplish the directive, the Mossad developed several assassination teams, each with specific mission parameters and methods of operation. The Mossad headquarters element developed one team utilizing staff operations officers supported by recruited assets of regional stations and managed through standard Mossad headquarters' procedures. A second unit recruited staff officers and highly trained specialists and set them outside the arm and control of the government. The theory was to support this team financially through covert mechanisms and let them operate with complete anonymity outside the government structure.

The assassination team deployed through normal channels failed to complete their mission and publicly exposed the entire operation. The second team which operated with full decentralized authority and freedom of movement achieved significant success in fulfilling their operational objectives and never compromised the operation.

Recommendations: Although there are inherent differences between Israeli and U.S. policies, specifically those addressing the use of assassination as a political tool, important lessons may be gleaned from this study for policy makers. Planners of sensitive covert operations must have a firm understanding of bureaucratic processes. Government bureaucracies inherently limit the degree of operational success by the nature of their systems. Bureaucracies cannot move effectively beyond a predetermined operational tempo, and impose fatal restraints regarding operational tradecraft and tactics. Successful covert operations demand a flexible capability with full decentralized authority enabling officers to initiate actions as circumstances dictate, enhancing the operational success-failure ratio.

When operational teams incorporate decentralized authority in concert with good trade craft and tactical techniques, success is virtually assured. Government agencies are capable of conducting decentralized, sensitive operations with reasonable operational control and an expectation of success.

ACKNOWLEDGMENTS

I would like to thank Mr. George Jonas for his candid conversation regarding Avner's team, which was so vital to this study. I would also like to give special thanks to my thesis advisor, Dr. James H. Anderson, my second mentor, Mr. N. Richard Kinsman, and my third reader and year-long faculty advisor, Dr. Donald F. Bittner. Additionally, I would like to acknowledge the military officers and civilian faculty of the U.S.M.C. University, Command and Staff College for allowing me the opportunity to participate in a unique learning experience.

CHAPTER 1
INTRODUCTION

THE EXPERIMENT

In 1972, the Israeli Mossad initiated one of the most ambitious covert counterterrorist campaigns in history. Golda Meir and the Israeli cabinet's top secret 'Committee-X' devised a campaign in retaliation for the massacre of eleven Israeli's during the Munich Olympic Games. Black September's (BSO) assault on the Olympic Village apartments on September 5, 1972, set in motion a chain of events unparalleled in the history of terrorism and antiterrorism tactics. Eleven Israeli's died in the assault at Olympic village and the subsequent failed (West) German police rescue attempt at Germany's Furstenfeldbruck airfield.

Outraged by intensifying PLO and BSO terrorist attacks on Israeli citizens, Prime Minister Golda Meir, with the support of her highest ranking cabinet officials, decided to take the war to the terrorists.

After the events of September 1972, Golda Meir authorized the formation of Mossad directed covert action teams to find and assassinate those individuals responsible for the attack on the Israeli athletes in Munich. This paper will explore the methods and concepts behind this counterterrorist effort, and analyze its success relative to the original operational objectives. Specifically, two case studies will demonstrate how the operational methodology as directed through the primary headquarters' element directly affected the level of success achieved by the teams outlined in the case studies. The specific concept of using assassination as a government tool is not the primary focus of the thesis. Rather, the research centers on the design of the teams, the operational objectives, to the field and had the option of a desk assignment. This did not appeal to Avner, as he was already very disillusioned with the Mossad leadership. He felt that they demanded absolute loyalty but did not return that loyalty. Mr. Jonas reported that to coerce him to stay, the Mossad blocked Avner's access to the Swiss bank account and threatened his family. Avner countered the threats and was recontacted by Harari soon after in an attempt to reconcile their disagreement.

The threats stopped, and Avner's money was still denied, but a resolution was eventually negotiated. Mr. Jonas commented that Avner "felt grievously betrayed at the end of the mission." 1 Avner was never led to believe that continued service in the Mossad was a condition for him to retrieve his promised salary. Money was not the original motivating factor for Avner for he had fully accepted the mission prior to the promise of the Swiss account. Avner had more contacts with the Mossad, however, the details of these encounters are not available.

In an attempt to start a new life, Avner teamed with Jonas to publish the accounts of the operations he conducted as chief of one of the most successfully orchestrated covert operations in history. Obviously, the name "Avner" is a pseudonym used to protect his true identity. Avner never identified Mike Harari by name for he utilized the pseudonym 'Ephraim' to identity his Mossad contact in his personal accounts as provided to Mr. Jonas. Harari was identified through later publications and the assumption that Ephraim was Harari was drawn through collateral research.

George Jonas is an accomplished author and currently produces movies and television shows for the Canadian Broadcasting Corporation in Toronto, Canada. Jonas explained the circumstances in which Avner came to his attention. At the conclusion of his mission and subsequent dispute with the Mossad, Avner contacted a British publishing company about his story. The publishing company in turn sought out the services of Jonas, well known and respected for his investigative journalistic skills, primarily in the law enforcement arena. Avner and Jonas discussed the possibilities of producing a book and the parameters of confidentiality. The two conducted a series of interviews regarding the details of Avner's mission to assassinate the top PLO terrorist leaders in Europe. Jonas related that Avner's recall of "small details" was remarkable. It was his ability to provide minute details inherent in the operations which enhanced Jonas' assessment of Avner's credibility. After discussing the events of the operations, Jonas traveled to the assassination sites to verify the accounts. Avner provided specifics of operational events which never appeared in news coverage of the assassinations. Only the few involved would have known the intricate operational tactics and movements described in depth by Avner. He produced detailed information regarding the movements and signals of the support teams, the makes and models of vehicles used, the descriptions of the assassination sites, weapons, the specially designed ammunition, the types of explosive devices, and their process of cultivating intelligence sources. 2

Jonas maintains his confidentiality pact with Avner regarding "Avner's" true identity. Open source published materials have speculated as to his true identify and his current location and occupation. The alleged Avner was contacted by this writer for his comments regarding the accounts in Jonas' book as well as his missions as a team leader with the Mossad. Avner related that the Mossad recently released an official statement confirming that the events published in Jonas' book, Vengeance, are, in fact, true. Contractual and confidentiality agreements prohibit him from making any further statements and or publicly confirming or denying "Avner's" true identity. Avner stated that the events in Jonas book are accurate and include all the detail he is willing, or contractually able, to provide. 3

Avner and Jonas refused to divulge the identities of the other officers involved in the operation. However, Avner assured Mr. Jonas that the personalities and specialties relating to each team member are accurate; hence, they are not composites to disguise the actual team.

Mike Harari and the names of the officers involved in the Lilleham-mer incident described in the first case study were identified and cross referenced through more recently published material. David B. Tinnin's book, The Hit Team, published in 1976, also provides an account of a team traveling through Europe assassinating PLO terrorists. Numerous discrepancies of tactical details of the operations exist between Tinnin's and Avner's accounts. Tinnin's premise of an independent team was correct, although his description of the team's personnel and operational tactics differed significantly from Avner's account. These discrepancies are discussed at length subsequent to the case studies in an effort to reconcile the differences. Also, the Mossad had commissioned numerous teams with different methods of operation. It is feasible that Tinnin had information regarding a third team, with a similar mission as Avner's, which was mentioned by Jonas..

CHAPTER 2
THE GAMBLE

MASSACRE AT MUNICH

At approximately 0400 hours on September 5, 1972, the "fedayeen" 1 (men of sacrifice) began executing their plan to scale the fences at Kusoczinskidamm, and capture the Israeli Olympic athletes residing at the Olympic Village apartments. The gunmen made their way to apartment one, at 31 Connollystrasse, Olympic Village Apartments, and inserted a passkey. Yossef Gutfreund, a 275 pound wrestling referee in apartment number one, began reacting to the sound of Arab voices behind his door. He quickly alerted his roommates there was danger and pushed his body against the door in an attempt to deny the Arab fedayeen entrance. Gutfreund's efforts were effective for only a few seconds, but allowed one roommate, weight lifting coach Tuvia Sokolovsky, time to break out a window and successfully escape. 2

The Arab terrorists successfully entered apartment one, immediately taking five Israeli team members hostage: track coach Amitzur Shapira, fencing master Andrei Spitzer, rifle coach Kehat Shorr, weightlifting judge Yacov Springer, and Yossef Gutfreund. The terrorists expanded their search throughout the complex, capturing six additional athletes in apartment number three. Wrestling coach Moshe Weinberger was away from the complex during the initial assault. He arrived back at the apartment while the terrorists continued their search for additional Israeli game participants. Upon entering the apartment, Weinberger struggled with two assassins, striking one and knocking him unconscious. The second Arab terrorist shot Weinberger in the face. Although critically wounded,

16

Weinberger rendered another attacker unconscious before being shot repeatedly in the chest by a third terrorist. Despite his efforts to defend himself and his colleagues, the Arab terrorists killed Weinberger with a point-blank gunshot to his head. 3

As the attack continued, weightlifter Yossef Romanno and teammate David Marc Berger tried to escape through an open kitchen window. Romanno, failing to make his way through the window, located a kitchen knife and stabbed one gunman in the forehead. A second Arab moved forward and fired from point blank range into Romanno with a Kalashnikov assault rifle, killing him. 4

By approximately 0500 hours, the Arab terrorists had killed two Israeli team members and captured nine. Due to the unanticipated battle and chaos, the terrorists failed to locate eight additional team members in apartments' two, four, and five. Two Israeli athletes had escaped and made their way to safety. Despite the gunfire, the activity at the Village Apartments drew very little notice from the other occupants in the area. The two athletes who escaped alerted the authorities to the incident. Within the next hour the Arab terrorists had issued a set of demands, written in English, and had thrown Moshe Weinberger's body into the street. 5

The Palestinian off-shoot group, the Black September Organization, claimed responsibility for the actions at the Village Apartments. Their demands included the release of 234 Arab and German prisoners held in Israel and West Germany. The terrorists provided a typewritten list of prisoners for release; these included Ulrike Meinhof and Andreas Baader, the founders and leaders of the German based Baader-Meinhof Gang. The German police had arrested both individuals earlier in June 1972. The terrorists also demanded that the police provide three planes for their escape. Upon receiving confirmation on the release of the prisoners, the terrorists would select one of the planes to transport them to a safe destination. 6

Frank Bolz, Jr., coauthor of The Counter-Terrorism Hand-book published in 1990, outlined the West German chain of command that coordinated the efforts to rescue the hostages. Manfred Schreiber, the Munich Police Commissioner, became the de-facto command authority over the hostage incident. Schreiber was also the officially appointed chief of the Olympic Security Forces. His superiors in Bonn established communications with Israel's Prime Minister, Golda Meir, as well as coordinated the possible release of the Baader-Meinhof Organization members with German authorities. The Interior Minister of Bavaria, Bruno Merk, acted as Schreiber's superior officer, and West German Chancellor Willy Brandt conducted discussions with the Israeli Prime Minister. Meir made it perfectly clear to Brandt that the Government of Israel would never negotiate with terrorists. 7

The West German police negotiators successfully extended three deadlines originally imposed by the terrorists. The Black September Group requested a jet to transport them to Cairo where the prisoners demanded for release by Israel would meet them. However, the government of Egypt refused to provide assistance in support of any West German police action during the crisis. This development, in combination with Golda Meir's absolute refusal to negotiate, forced Schreiber to conclude that a rescue attempt was his only option. Schreiber determined that in order to conduct a successful hostage rescue, he must confine the terrorists to Germany. To initiate a rescue, he decided the best option was to isolate the terrorists at Germany's Furstenfeldbruck Airport. Once at the airfield, West German sharpshooters would attempt a hostage rescue operation. 8

It is important to note that Mossad Chief Zwi Zamir had traveled directly to Munich, on orders from Golda Meir, to discuss the ongoing incident with the West German authorities. Golda Meir had directed him to negotiate permission for specially trained Israeli commandos, the 'sayeret,' to conduct the hostage rescue. The sayeret are elite trained reconnaissance forces drawn from the ranks of the Israeli Special Forces and experienced in hostage rescue techniques. Although Chancellor Brandt might have acquiesced, the local state officials refused. According to the German federal constitution, the decision was in the hands of the state officials. Unfortunately the German police lacked the expertise and experience of the Israeli sayeret. 9 It was only after the arrival at the airport that the West German Police realized there were eight terrorist members, not the five originally estimated. Considering the early estimate of five terrorists, the police deployed only five German snipers at Furstenfeldbruck airport to initiate the rescue. This was far short of the sniper requirements for this type of ambush scenario. The German police also placed a dummy Lufthansa Boeing 727 at Furstenfeldbruck airport, located approximately fifteen miles from the center of Munich. Eight police officers deployed around the jet dressed as flight attendants and crew members. Unfortunately these police officers were without radio contact with the command post or other police units. 10

As the terrorists moved a 'safe' distance from the hostages, Schreiber ordered the police snipers to open fire. Their initial rounds went off-target and a full gun battle ensued. The Israeli captives were still sitting bound in the helicopters which had transported them to the airfield. The initial fire fight between the fedayeen and police lasted approximately an hour and fifteen minutes. The German Police decided to initiate an 'infantry' attack to move the terrorists from the vicinity of the helicopters. As the attack began, one fedayeen tossed a grenade into one of the helicopters holding five of the Israeli athletes. The helicopter exploded, killing all five athletes. Shortly thereafter, another fedayeen member entered the second helicopter, shot, and killed the last four hostages. The police captured three terrorists during the ensuing fire fight. At approximately 0130 hours, the police killed the last of the Arab terrorists. 11 The German police investigation indicated that a few of the hostages may have inadvertently been shot by the German police during the fierce gun battle. However, a definitive conclusion was not possible due to the severely burned condition of the bodies. 12

Although it is clearly evident that many things went wrong in the hostage rescue attempt, it is not the purpose of this paper to explore those factors. However, there are a number of important issues for consideration which became apparent after the failed rescue effort. According to 1972 Facts on File, the West German police identified Yossef Gutfreund and Yacov Springer as Israeli security agents posing as Olympic team members. The three captured Arab terrorists confessed that they were students who had recently lived in Jordan. They also disclosed that there were possibly fifteen Arab guerrillas plotting additional terrorist attacks. What is paramount is the reaction of the Israeli Government to this incident. The West German Police were very critical of Golda Meir's absolute resistance to cooperate in any negotiations with the terrorists to effect the release of the hostages. Israel's history contains countless incidents of terrorist tactics employed by her enemies. Golda Meir, in an official statement, warned that "Israel will persevere in her struggle against the terrorist organizations and will not absolve their accomplices from responsibility for terrorist actions." 13 Unnamed Israeli sources later identified those countries as Egypt, Syria, and Lebanon. The Egyptian official reaction accused the West German police of making false charges against Egypt regarding a lack of cooperation. Egyptian officials also placed responsibility of the deaths of the hostages on the West German police, claiming that it was their bullets that killed the hostages.

The Black September Organization

A Palestinian guerrilla group, The Black September Organization (BSO), claimed responsibility for the killing of the eleven Israeli's in Munich. The Fatah originated in 1957 and boasted an estimated membership of over 11,000 by the late 1980's. The United States Department of State's 1988 publication of Terrorist Group Profiles, describes the Fatah as the military arm of the Palestine Liberation Organization (PLO). Fatah is an acronym spelled backwards representing Harakat al-Tahrir al Filistini. The phrase translates as Palestine Liberation Movement. Former Fatah leader Yasir Arafat (Abu Ammar) assumed leadership of the PLO in 1969. The Fatah utilized the name Black September Organization from approximately 1971 to 1974. Some sources speculate that Arafat utilized the name to distance himself and the PLO from the actions of the BSO. Many terrorist experts speculate that Arafat controlled the BSO and utilized it as his primary military force. Arafat attempted to keep the association at arm's length to provide a factor of plausible deniability. Black September represents the results of the culmination of tensions between the Fatah and the Jordanian government. In September 1970, King Hussein's military forced the group out of Jordan and into Lebanon.

The expulsion of Fatah from Jordan and Egypt severely limited the group's ability to launch cross-border operations into Israel. Thus, the Fatah resorted to increased terrorist activities as a means to attack Israel. Black September conducted nine major terrorist attacks in 1971 and early 1972 prior to the Munich Olympic incident. On September 6, 1971, the London Times reported that the BSO had been in contact with the Baader-Meinhof terrorist group in West Germany. In addition, the London Times reported that Andreas Baader met secretly in Beirut with Palestinian officials in February 1971, prior to his arrest. 14 However, there was no specific information regarding possible agreements between the two groups.

Also, five days after the Munich incident, an Israeli recruited agent ambushed case officer Zadok Ofir in Brussels. Ofir was working under official cover as the First Secretary at the Israeli Embassy in Brussels. He received an urgent phone call from his agent claiming that an emergency meeting was necessary. The agent was an Arab traveling on a Moroccan passport. At a meeting set at the Cafe Prince, Ofir's recruited agent shot him in the abdomen at point blank range. Ofir survived the shooting and the ensuing investigation determined that the individual Ofir went to meet was a double agent and an active member of the BSO. 15

CHAPTER 3
ISRAEL RESPONDS

GOLDA MEIR AND COMMITTEE-X

The results of the failed rescue mission in Germany caused Israeli Premier Golda Meir great distress. The reluctance of German police to utilize experienced Israeli commandos in the rescue attempt also disappointed Meir. However, she publicly praised the West German police for taking aggressive action against the fedayeen in Munich and encouraged other countries to follow suit. 1 Israel maintained then, and still does, that a 'no compromise' stance is the only viable solution in stemming terrorist aggression.

As a result of the Munich incident, in conjunction with growing BSO terrorist activities, Golda Meir developed a new counterterrorism policy. General Aharon Yariv accepted the new position of the Prime Minister's Advisor on Counterterrorism. Golda Meir, General Yariv, and Mossad Chief General Zwi Zamir also persuaded the Israeli Cabinet to form a top secret counterterrorist committee. Meir tasked the committee with devising an appropriate response to the Munich massacre. Golda Meir and Defense Minister Moshe Dayan chaired the special panel, known simply as "Committee-X." 2 (According to Dan Raviv and Yossi Melman, authors of Every Spy a Prince, the journalist, Yoel Marcus, was the first to expose the activities of "Committee X" in Har'aretz on June 10, 1986.) The panel concluded that the most effective means to make a clear statement that Israel would not tolerate terrorist activity was to authorize the assassination of any Black September terrorists involved in the Munich incident.

23

This directive included any individual identified as either directly or indirectly involved in the planning or the execution of the assault on the Israeli athletes in Munich.

Committee-X assigned the Mossad the task of implementing the panel's directive. The committee made it clear to the Mossad leadership that the objective was to kill the BSO members and create terror within the terrorists' organizations. It was not a mission devised to capture and/or prosecute suspects. Mossad Chief Zwi Zamir appointed senior agent Mike Harari to oversee the development of the special covert action teams. Harari worked in conjunction with a Mossad operations officer, Abraham Gehmer, who worked under official cover as the First Secretary of the Israeli Embassy in Paris. The Mossad established Paris as their regional base for European operations. 3

CASE STUDIES

In order to implement the directive issued by Golda Meir's Committee X, Harari and his superiors chose an unusual but historic approach. Harari formed several assassination teams, each with specific mission parameters and methods of operation. The panel tightly compartmentalized the teams to the point that the teams were unaware of one another. The Mossad intended to succeed in achieving the panel's, and particularly Golda Meir's, objectives. In this respect they attacked the problem from varied angles, hoping to develop an interlocking information net which terrorist targets would be unable to avoid. If one method was ineffective or missed a lead, another team would probably fill the gap.

Two particular units are described in this paper which represent two different methods of personnel recruitment, headquarters control, support, and intervention. The success of these teams becomes apparent through close examination of their methodologies. The Mossad head-quarters element developed one team utilizing staff operations officers supported by recruited assets of regional stations and managed through standard Mossad headquarters' procedures; one of these is depicted in the "Lillehammer" case study. The second unit recruited staff officers and highly trained specialists and set them outside the arm and control of the government; this is the "Avner" group case study. The theory was to covertly support this team financially and let them operate with complete anonymity outside the government structure. Their only contact was with Harari, established through covert signals and then only on rare occasions. Harari provided the unit a list of target names and instructions for obtaining funds through covert accounts prior to deployment.

As described earlier, the details of Avner's covert action team in the second case study is primarily derived from George Jonas' book, Vengeance. Avner, a former Mossad officer is the principal source of information detailing the team's operations. Although the Israeli Government has acknowledged that covert teams were deployed after the Munich incident to assassinate PLO terrorists, official details regarding the teams' actual methods remain classified. Considering the nature of the mission, it is doubtful that any absolute official evidence of the assassination program exists. Newspaper reports, investigative reports, police reports, and unclassified United States government files all verify the assassinations of the PLO terrorists. Many western journalists also speculated that the assassinations were conducted by the Israeli "Wrath of God" assassination teams. It is debatable whether the Mossad actually used the term "Wrath of God," or if the media attached the title. It may also have been utilized by Israeli propaganda specialists to increase PLO paranoia. 4 Former officers of the Mossad have also verified the firearms methodology utilized by Mossad specialists, to include their preference for the Baretta .22 caliber pistol. These officers also acknowledged that the Mossad incorporated an internal assassination section.

LILLEHAMMER

The first case examines the details of the attempted assassination of Ali Hassan Salameh in Lillehammer on July 21, 1973. This operation resulted in the exposure of seven Israeli officers in a highly publicized media event. The operation was clearly a failure for a myriad of reasons. This case, however, examines the elements of a sensitive operation coordinated and implemented though headquarters procedures and the inherent problems in such an operation.

Harari was the controlling officer for the mission to assassinate BSO leader Ali Hassan Salameh, the primary architect of the Munich massacre, and the Mossad's number one target. Numerous publications have identified Harari as the chief of the Lillehammer operation. Victor Ostrovsky, a former Mossad Staff Operations officer from approximately January 1983 to 1987 and coauthor of By Way of Deception, (1990) specifically identified Harari as the Chief of the Metsada. He defined the Metsada as a highly secret organization within the Mossad which operates combatants. Within the Metsada is the "Kidon," a specially trained, elite assassination unit. According to Ostrovsky, kidon is a translation of the word 'bayonet,' and is the operational arm of the Mossad responsible for kidnappings and executions. 5 Ostrovsky also commented that after his recruitment into the Mossad, he learned he was being groomed for the Kidon.

After a year of searching and following endless erroneous leads, the Mossad finally acquired confirmed intelligence placing Salameh in Lillehammer, Norway. The Mossad wanted to seize the opportunity and act immediately on this information. General Zwi Zamir, the Mossad Chief, was monitoring the developments in Israel while Harari developed and deployed the assassination team. Harari selected five Mossad staff officers as the primary engagement unit for the operation. The action element included Dan Arbel, Abraham Gehmer, Zwi Steinberg, Michael Dorf, and Yigal Zigal. It seems odd that since the Mossad incorporates a special unit to conduct these operations, that Harari did not choose to deploy an established kidon unit for the assignment. The support team, composed of regionally recruited assets including Marriane Gladnikoff, conducted the necessary surveillance of Salameh and monitored his movements. In addition, they established safe houses and acquired the vehicles required for the "action" unit. 6

The culmination of this mission occurred in July 1973, more than a year after the reported initial deployment of the assassination teams. On July 21, 1973, the Israeli assassination team shot and killed an innocent man closely resembling Salameh. Earlier that day the surveillance team followed the individual they believed to be Salameh to a local public swimming pool. Soon after, he exited with an obviously pregnant woman. At approximately 1400 hours, the assassination team arrived in-country and proceeded to the Oppland Tourist Hotel where they registered under alias names. The surveillance team reported that they observed the assumed Salameh enter a movie theater with the same pregnant woman at approximately 2000 hours. The action team departed the hotel and deployed to intercept the target after he left the theater. The target and female companion excited the movie at approximately 2235 hours and took a bus to an area just a "short walk" from their flat. As they began their walk from the bus stop to the flat, two members of the action team exited a Mazda and began firing into the man believed to be Salameh with Baretta .22 caliber pistols. The pregnant woman crouched over the dying man, screaming as the team escaped from the scene. Individuals in the neighborhood notified the police, who arrived at the scene within the next few minutes. The team dropped the Mazda at a predesignated point and transferred to a Peugeot rented from a Scandinavian rental company to transport them out of Lillehammer.7

The authorities identified the dead man as Ahmed Bouchiki, a Moroccan, working as a waiter in Lillehammer. The pregnant woman was later identified as Bouchiki's wife. The police observed the Peugeot with the assassination team on a road leading away from Lillehammer after receiving reports of the shooting. Unfortunately, Dan Arbel and Marrianne Gladnikoff used poor operational trade craft and utilized the Peugeot a second time to travel to the airport 24 hours later. Airport personnel observed the vehicle and reported it to the police. The police located the vehicle and immediately arrested both occupants.

During the police interrogation, Gladnikoff provided the police a safe house address as her residence. She also broke down and reported that she was working for the Government of Israel. Arbel had an unlisted phone number in his possession which lead the police to Yigal Zigal, originally believed to be an employee of El Al Airlines. Following Gladnikoff's lead, the police responded to the safe house address and discovered Yigal Zigal, Zwi Steinberg and Michael Dorf. Zigal claimed to be an Israeli Security Officer assigned to the Israeli embassy. He offered the police official Israeli credentials at the time of his arrest, ordered the police to leave the apartment, and attempted to claim diplomatic immunity. The police disregarded the credentials and took Zigal, Dorf, and Steinberg into custody. The police also discovered a detailed Mossad cable of instructions in Dorf's possession identifying the Mossad and specific evacuation procedures. This cable specifically ordered the unit not to carry any potentially compromising material with them during the course of the operation. 8 Steinberg also had two keys with a blue label attached identifying an apartment in Paris. After official notification, the French police responded to the address identified on the key labels. The French located the apartment and identified it as another Israeli safe house. Within that apartment were more keys and labels exposing almost every safe house in Paris. The French authorities recovered other incriminating evidence that allegedly linked the Israeli Government with other assassinations of PLO terrorists. A public trial of the six arrested Israeli team members exposed the details of the operation. Five team members were convicted for killing the waiter; Michael Dorf was acquitted. 9 Dan Raviv, coauthor of Every Spy a Prince, reported that although the five officers were sentenced from two to five and one-half years in prison, all five were released by the Norwegians in less than twenty-two months.

AVNER

The second case examines an independent team organized by Mike Harari. Unless otherwise noted, the account of Avner's team was drawn from George Jonas' book, Vengeance (1984). The pseudonym "Avner" represents the unit team leader selected by Harari for the operation. 10 Avner's unit consisted of five highly trained individuals with varied specialties. Each officer had some second and third language proficiency. The different specialties included: devising alias documents, appropriating vehicles, improvised explosive devices (IED), small arms, electronics, business, banking, and operational security. The premise of the unit was total flexibility. Although each officer had specialized skills, each team member could essentially perform any task.

The design of the unit closely resembled United States Army special forces' units. The members formed a team without utilizing rank and formal military doctrine. It was absolutely essential that the unit operate informally while creating and implementing operational plans. Falling into formal military protocol during an operation could prove fatal. Avner did not want to limit his team's flexibility with a rigid chain of command. Also, Avner understood that as the unit chief, he could not afford to isolate himself from his team in an assignment of extended duration.

Harari explained that the philosophy of Avner's operation was to cut off the leaders from their organization. Because terrorist groups are "unlike military forces ... and have no life power of their own ... they must be supplied with everything they need for survival; money, weapons, papers, hideouts, training, and recruits." With their "lifeline severed, a whole network of them will disappear." 11 The objective of the entire operation was to sever the leadership and throw the organization into chaos. Of course, the organizations could rebuild; however, this would require time. The Mossad hoped to identify the new leaders during that rebuilding process and seek further opportunities to neutralize that progress.

To sever any official ties with the Israeli Government, Avner's team resigned from their positions in the Mossad. With no formal contractual agreements, the resignations effectively terminated any further paper trails'. Due to the lack of open source conclusive evidence, absolute verification that all the team members actually served with the Mossad prior to this mission is not possible. Published materials have protected the identities of members of this team. However, their specialized skills, in concert with their understanding of covert operational trade craft, would indicate intelligence association of some form. The selection of the team members was critical in matching personalities and specialties. Harari emphasized the critical aspect of the permanency of the unit. The unit would not substitute officers during the course of the operation. The unit would operate until the successful completion of the mission or until death or injuries rendered it inoperable. The concept was for the team to combine their specialties into a totally flexible lethal unit.

General Zwi Zamir provided the team with a list of priority targets, which included the following: 12

Ali Hassan Salameh

Developed and executed the assault on the Israeli athletes at Olympic Village;

Abu Daoud

Arrested in Germany, March 1973; confessed to his involvement in Munich; admitted member of the BSO, directed by Fatah leader Yassar;

Mohmoud Hamshari

PLO member and coordinator of Munich incident;

Wael Zwaiter, a.k.a., Abdel Wael Zuaiter

Arafat's 2nd cousin, organizer of terrorism in Europe;

Dr. Basil Raoud al-Kubaisi, a.k.a., Bassel Rauf Kubeisy

Coordinated logistics for the Popular Front for the Liberation of Palestine;

Kamal Nasser

Official spokesman for the PLO;

Kemal Adwan

Chief of sabotage operations for Al Fatah in Israeli occupied territories;

Abu Yussuf, a.k.a., Mahmoud Yussuf Najjer

High ranking PLO official;

Mohammed Boudia

Linked with European PLO;

Hussein Abad al-Chir

PLO contact with KGB in Cyprus;

Dr. Wadi Haddad

Chief terrorist linked with Dr. George Habash.

Prior to deployment, Harari brought the team together in Israel for a few days of "refresher courses" and in-depth briefings regarding the Mossad's current intelligence on each target. The Mossad also provided official passports for their initial deployment to Geneva, where they would set up their first temporary operational base. They would then lock away any personal items and official passports for the duration of the mission.

Harari provided the team with only two principle rules of engagement prior to their deployment. The Mossad's intent was to send a message with every assassination that PLO terrorists could not hide from Israel under any circumstances. He wanted the team to be imaginative and strike in creative ways. In this vein, the terrorists would know that they had been "touched." If the assassinations occurred while the terrorist leaders operated within their own security nets, it would send a clear message that they would never feel safe. The second principle was for the team to act with zero collateral risk. Harari made it clear that the unit was to ensure one hundred percent identification of the target before acting. Harari did not want his covert action unit to act with the same recklessness and disregard of innocents as the terrorists they were hunting. If the unit could not obtain absolute identification, they were to abort the mission and attempt the "hit" again at a later time. He emphasized that if the team killed only three terrorists, the mission is a success, although disappointing. However, if the unit killed all eleven on the list but also killed one innocent, the mission would be a failure. 13 This was the entirety of the team's headquarters' guidance regarding operations and rules of engagement. Ironically, these precepts were set almost a year prior to the failed Lillehammer incident which was coordinated by Harari.

The first order of business in Geneva was to determine "hard" and "soft" targets. Hard targets represented individuals who might be utilizing security teams, disguises, and varied routines, and/or carrying weapons. Hard targets operate at a higher clandestine sophistication level and are generally alert to sting operations and surveillance. To protect themselves, they utilize covert 'trade craft' and change their schedules frequently. Soft targets are the individuals who do not hide their sympathies to the Palestinian cause and lived routine open lifestyles. Their daily activities were predictable and did not include security measures. These targets only operated in a clandestine capacity part time. Soft targets were more accessible and required much less effort in acquiring positive identification. 14

The team's first operational priority was to acquire recent accurate information on the movements of the targets on the list. Without solid leads to begin their operation, Avner decided to disperse the team throughout Europe. Each individual targeted regions with which he was familiar and had established contacts. Each member would expand the network of contacts in his region and develop "sources" of reliable information to support the mission. It was necessary to create a foundation from which to operate. This included target intelligence, weapons, documents and support personnel.

In the early stages, Avner developed a source who was trying to make his way into the higher echelon of the Baader-Meinhof Red Army Faction. He believed that introducing Avner's readily available cash flow to the group might increase his own value. Avner's source assumed Avner and his partners had embezzled a great deal of money and were possibly funding a small independent terrorist unit. Even if this were the case, he did not inquire further because the Baader-Meinhof Organization was always seeking new sources of hard currency to fund their activities. The source believed if he could produce substantial ready cash from Avner, it would elevate his status within the organization. As a result, the Baader-Meinhof organization provided basic preliminary logistical support for Avner's early operations, while allowing him the opportunity to begin establishing his underground identity and bona-fides. In order to operate effectively and obtain peripheral support, Avner had to establish an effective cover which would withstand close scrutiny. This required having key individuals and/or organizations vouch for his authenticity; Baader-Meinhof provided the foundation for Avner's acceptance in the underground terrorist networks. Avner's team utilized the Baader-Meinhof association in the early stages of the mission to cultivate a working network of sources.

The team reconvened in Geneva to consolidate their information. After careful analysis, they selected Wael Zwaiter as their first target. The group determined that Zwaiter was a soft target, living and operating in Rome. The squad traveled separately to Italy and rendezvoused in Ostia, an area a few miles outside Rome where they secured sleeping quarters at three different sites. The weapons specialist made arrangements to have five Baretta .22 caliber, semi-automatic pistols with extra ammunition and magazines transported into Italy through his own established network of arms' suppliers. The Baader-Meinhof group provided Avner with personnel for operational support and target surveillance. The support assets reported all Zwaiter's movements and daily routine. These assets were unaware of the actual mission and would not be present during the actual hit.

On October 16, 1972, a vehicle driven by a support team member delivered Avner and one additional "shooter" to the vicinity of Zwaiter's apartment complex and exited the area. A third action member occupied the passenger seat of a vehicle operated by a female support asset, also in close proximity. The female was responsible for signaling the group of Zwaiter's approach. As an advance team approached the area, the female's passenger would exit the vehicle and she would drive away from the site, signaling the team that the target was approaching and the operation was a "go."

The female said good-bye to her passenger and drove away as the team moved into their rehearsed positions. Another couple from the support team advanced Zwaiter's movements by approximately one minute. A blond female ran to join the advance couple and they strolled away from the apartment complex; the final signal that Zwaiter was approaching alone. The two shooters entered the complex ahead of the target to set themselves in position in the lobby. Avner had conducted an advance (recon) earlier to familiarize himself with the interior of the lobby and develop contingency plans. As expected, Zwaiter stopped for a few minutes at a tavern across from the apartment complex to make a phone call. The surveillance team had learned that the local phone company had disconnected Zwaiter's phone service for lack of payment. Surveillance reports also indicated that Zwaiter would routinely stop at the tavern enroute to his apartment to make phone calls.

After completing his call, Zwaiter continued towards his apartment on schedule. The lobby was dimly lit and, as Zwaiter entered, Avner switched on additional lights to positively identify his target. As Zwaiter looked up from something held in his hands, a bit confused at the light, the second shooter asked the target if he was Wael Zwaiter. With positive identification established, the two commandos quickly drew their weapons and shot fourteen rounds (custom designed .22 caliber bullets) into Zwaiter. The two exited through the main lobby entrance where two teammates were waiting in a vehicle to transport them from the area. The fifth unit member's job was about to begin. He was the security man who would go back into the scene and "sweep" it for any incriminating evidence accidentally left behind by anyone involved in the action. The team drove to a predesignated area and transferred to a van operated by another support asset who transported the unit to a safe house. The team had successfully accomplished their first mission. The cost to the Mossad for the operation was approximately $350,000 dollars.

Following the Zwaiter operation in Rome, Avner's Baader-Meinhof contact introduced him a new source of information in Paris. Avner's team had established itself as a bona-fide mercenary group buying and selling information on terrorists. Their access to quick large sums of cash opened doors with few questions asked. Following their first operation, Avner secured an introduction to "Louis," a member of a free lance information organization known only as "Le Group." 15 Papa, Louis' father, was a former member of the French Resistance during World War II and the originator of Le Group.

The organization essentially grew out of the French Resistance, and was predicated on the premise that there would always be a demand for services and material for various groups seeking the means to further their cause. Papa devised a "private" underground intelligence service which provided information, weapons, documents, clothing, surveillance teams, vehicles, safe houses, etc., to individuals seeking such services with extreme discretion and few questions asked. The primary condition for the services of Le Group was hard currency. Papa's only restriction was that he would not provide services to an official government entity. He felt governments were simply too "treacherous and unscrupulous ... and riddled with politics." 16

Le Group provided the information required by Avner's team for their next selected target, Mahmoud Hamshari. Avner wanted a more spectacular means for this "hit" to encapsulate Harari's directive of shaking up the terrorist with their "reach." Le Group deployed a surveillance team which reported on Hamshari's routine. One team member acting as an Italian Journalist contacted Hamshari via telephone and suggested a meeting for an interview. After Hamshari acknowledged his interest in such a meeting, the caller advised him that he would be contacted in several days to make the appropriate arrangements. This was a ploy to have Hamshari positively identify himself on the phone. The action team planned to wire the base of the telephone with explosives which they would initiate through a remote triggering device.

Avner and his unit went through their routine of running rehearsals, advances, and signals prior to the operation. Everything was in place on December 8, 1972. Hamshari sat alone in his apartment awaiting the phone call from the Italian journalist. The team received their "go" signal and the explosives' specialist detonated the explosives. The unit was successful again.

Le Group would provide all the necessary support to Avner's team for the next four independent missions; Abad al-Chir, Basil al-Kubaisi, Zaid Muchassi, and Mohammed Boudia. 17 The specific details of each operation are not required for the purposes of this paper; only that each was conducted methodically and was successful without compromise to the team. Although not on the original list, Muchassi was Abad al-Chir's replacement as the PLO contact with the Soviet Union's KGB. After receiving reliable information on Muchassi from Le Group, Avner's team made a unilateral decision to include him in their mission.

The team decided that if Abad al-Chir had been selected as a target, it was reasonable to believe that his replacement was also a viable target. The Mossad always taught its officers to use initiative and make reasonable decisions in the field. Avner's team had acquired the information required for an operation targeting Muchassi and had the opportunity and the means. Unfortunately, during this operation, Avner's team encountered Muchassi's KGB contact officer in a vehicle blocking the path of their escape. The team shot and killed the KGB officer after observing him reach for a weapon under his jacket.

In March 1973, Harari contacted Avner's unit regarding a change in procedure. Harari was aware that Avner and his unit had acquired significant success in obtaining intelligence on PLO terrorists. Harari's had received intelligence that three targets on the original list were meeting in Beirut. He advised Avner that Mahmoud Yussuf Najjer, Kamal Nasser, and Kemal Adwan were no longer on his target list. Harari wanted Avner's team to provide their intelligence and sources to him in support of a Mossad directed military action in Beirut. The military action would include the killing of the three terrorists as well as other objectives within a single orchestrated operation.

Avner was extremely tentative about turning over Le Group to the Mossad, especially after Papa had made it clear that he would not support organized government operations. Avner was extremely concerned about losing Le Group's services, as well as jeopardizing the security of his unit. He informed Harari that he would not divulge his sources. Avner and Harari designed a compromise to protect Le Group yet utilize their service to perform the advance, surveillance and intelligence for the operation. The Mossad, in conjunction with the Israeli Defense Forces (IDF), would perform the actual mission.

In April 1973, forty Israeli commandos conducted a covert amphibious landing on a Beirut beach setting in motion an ambitious mission to strike at multiple targets and deliver a decisive blow against the PLO. The operation succeeded in killing Adwan, Najjer, and Nasser, as well as approximately one hundred PLO Guerrillas. However, it also included two innocent casualties: Najjer's wife and one neighbor. Najjer's wife had moved in front of Najjer in an attempt to shield him from fire. During the commotion, the neighbor opened her door out of curiosity and was killed by Israeli commandos. The Israeli's reported one dead and three wounded during the assault. The overall mission was a tremendous success. 18

In late 1973, Avner's team learned of the Salameh incident in Lille-hammer and realized for the first time that Harari was using other teams to target the same PLO terrorists as his list. Harari never disclosed to the unit that any other teams, whether controlled through Mossad headquarters or independent, were also involved in the same mission.

In January 1974, Avner's unit received information of Salameh's presence in Sargans, near Liechtenstein, Switzerland. Salameh was reportedly going to meet other PLO leaders in a church on January 12, 1974. After contemplating a number of alternative plans, they concluded that an attack inside the church was the most feasible. Avner and his partner entered the dark church and encountered three armed Arabs. As one young Arab reached for a pistol, Avner and his partner quickly reacted by shooting the three men. They continued down the church stairs toward the basement where they encountered three very startled and obviously frightened priests. A third team member then watched the priests as the two primary shooters went back up the stairs to continue the search for Salameh. As the mission unraveled, Avner made the decision to abort the operation and move to the escape phase. This was the first failure of the unit and included the possible deaths of three Arabs not on their list. Avner's team was distressed over the engagement with the three guards, however, the unit felt justified in their actions in that the Arabs' were clearly combatants, not innocents. This second attempt on Salameh had failed, but, Avner's team avoided compromise or arrest.

As the mission continued, in May 1974, the team found themselves in London, England. Avner was attempting contact with a source with possible information regarding Salameh. His source never made the prear-ranged meeting. Avner felt uncomfortable about the aborted meeting, and also mentioned to the group that he believed he was under surveillance.

He related his concern that the British authorities may have discovered their presence in the capital and were conducting surveillance operations against the team. Only three team members were in London, where they had hoped to conclude their business in three to four days then meet the other two back in Frankfurt. Avner and one partner were staying at the Europa Hotel. One evening after dinner, Avner decided to spend some leisure time in the Etruscan Bar. A very attractive blond woman enticed Avner into a conversation for a short time at the bar. As Avner left the woman and the bar en route to his room, he passed his partner heading to the bar for a drink. After a short time, Avner went back to the bar to socialize with his partner but observed that both he and the woman had departed.

Avner and his teammate had separate bedrooms which shared a common foyer. As Avner went into his room he noticed the same strong perfume of the woman at the bar and heard the sound of a female laughing in his partner's room. The next morning Avner's partner failed to arrive for breakfast. Concerned, Avner went to his partner's room to check on his welfare. After receiving no response to his knocks on the door, Avner entered the room. He found his partner dead, lying naked on the bed with a bullet wound to the chest. Avner contacted Le Group, which handled all the details of sanitizing the room and disposing of the body. Avner also asked Le Group to provide him any information they could obtain regarding the woman's identity.

After arriving in Frankfurt, Avner provided the details of the death to the other team members. After reviewing the information provided by Le Group, the team uniformly agreed to track and assassinate the responsible woman. Although this was a clear disregard of their mission parameters, the emotional impact of the incident pushed them to pursue the woman. Le Group had determined that the woman was a free lance assassin whom Avner had positively identified through photographs obtained by Le Group. Her services were available to any one willing to meet her fees. The woman resided in Hoorn, just outside Amsterdam. On August 21, 1974, the team conducted a mission to assassinate the woman in the same fashion as their previous operations. As the assassination team approached her, the woman instinctively reached for a weapon. The team subsequently shot and killed her. 19 There was no information available as to who had contracted her services for the hit on Avner's team. Mr. Jonas reported that Avner was severely reprimanded for acting unilaterally in assassinating the woman. This was clearly outside the parameters initially established by Harari for team operations. 20

On September 14, 1974, another team member was killed while making contact with a source associated with his Belgium weapons connection. Again, Le Group provided all the necessary services to dispose of the body. Avner had been asked numerous times if he thought Le Group had betrayed the unit and provided other interest's information regarding Avner's team. Avner maintains his position that Le Group never betrayed the team. Mr. Jonas commented that he questioned Avner specifically on this issue. According to Mr. Jonas, Avner clearly understood Le Group's business philosophy that hard currency buys services. However, Avner believed Papa was loyal to him in that there were many opportunities throughout their relationship where Papa could have betrayed the team and did not.

Harari directed the team to abandon the mission after the second death in the team. Avner and the team made the decision not to acknowledge Harari's message and try one more time for Salameh in Tarifa, along the Gibraltar Atlantic coast. Salameh was reportedly in a house "on top of some low cliffs lining the beach." 21 On October 10, 1974, Avner's remaining team of three attempted their last operation. They chose a commando style infiltration to gain access to the house. During the infiltration phase, the team encountered an Arab security man with a Kalashnikov assault rifle and subsequently killed him. Again, the plan was unraveling and Avner aborted the operation. This was the end of their two year quest to hunt PLO terrorists. 22

Avner's team had deployed almost two years earlier with a list of eleven PLO terrorists. Throughout this period his team succeeded in terminating eight of the original eleven and one replacement PLO leader outside the list. The collateral damage assessment included: one KGB officer, four PLO security men, one free lance assassin, and two team members.

CHAPTER 4
ANALYSIS AND CONCLUSION

ORGANIZATIONS AND THE HUMAN CONDITION

Harari's method of deploying numerous teams simultaneously with different methodologies to attack the PLO problem was innovative. Golda Meir issued a difficult directive to achieve. It was Harari's responsibility to assassinate top PLO terrorists while ensuring zero collateral risk. He also needed to protect the Mossad with a reasonable degree of deniability associated with those assassinations. Only Golda Meir's Committee-X had a full understanding of the operation. Harari struggled with deploying teams to assassinate PLO terrorists without associating the Mossad with the actions. He also needed to screen the operation from the senior members of the cabinet outside of Committee-X. He was under pressure to take both official and unofficial actions against the PLO.

According to Victor Ostrovsky, By Way of Deception, the Mossad had the required mechanisms within the "Metsada" branch to execute kidnapping and assassinations. Further, the Mossad's written charter allows the Mossad discretionary authority to conduct assassinations. Ostrovsky explained that the unit designated for such assignments is the "Kidon." Three teams of twelve individuals each comprised one unit. Generally two teams conduct training in Israel while the third team deploys abroad. These teams remain separated from the other Mossad members, and are not briefed on personnel, structure, or operations outside their unit. The members of the assassination teams use aliases even within their own environment to ensure the true identities of the individuals remain secure. 1

Harari utilized all the assets at his disposal as opportunities arose. Avner's team deployed as an independent entity, allowing them to operate at their own pace. However, when pressure was building from the Israeli Cabinet to take some sort official action he combined his resources and initiated the Mossad-IDF operation in Beirut. When Mossad intelligence verified Salameh's location in Lillehammer, Harari assembled an improvised team to respond immediately, but this operation ended in disaster: the mission resulted in the killing of the wrong person and the arrest of six Israeli officers.

Developing another team with the freedom to move outside the control and policy of the government was an extremely bold and risky proposition. However, Harari had the insight to understand that a team unburdened by a slow moving bureaucratic process had the capability of moving with more efficiency and success. If designed correctly, the Mossad would keep an acceptable level of plausible deniability in their association with the team.

Geoffrey M. Bellman, author of The Consultant's Calling, is an expert on organizational structure and functionality. He explains why an organization is only capable of performing to a certain level of mediocrity. Organizational structure is essential to conducting business in a modern complex society. However, it is important to understand the dynamics and limitations of an organization. Bellman relates that organizations are:

Large, awkward, and unwieldy. Usually organizations don't work very well because they don't fit the human creatures who work in them. Organizations as we have built them are more mechanical than 'organic'... we have built awkward hierarchical structures with boxes and lines connecting them. We have created structures modeled after machines--mechanistic, sharply defined, and inflexible--that force their moving human parts to act like machines too. Such organizations do not work very well ... even when everything is finely in tune ... there are significant difficulties. 2

This concept illustrates the dynamics of an organization relative to the decision making process. It also highlights that inherent limitations exist in every system. The organization is essential to conduct business in the world. To truly succeed, those functioning within organizations must understand the limitations of the system and determine accurate estimates of success relative to those limitations. Are the objectives set forth by the command or supervisory element actually achievable within the policies of the organization? Also, does the directive fall within the inherent limitations of the system itself? Bellman maintains that:

important organizational decisions are not made because they are logical and rational. Logic and rationality are used in support of the decision, as kind of psychic insurance. Organizations swing through cycles of centralization and decentralization, and they don't do it because it makes sense. CEO's select executives who are first loyal and only secondarily have managerial competence. Much of business does not make sense, and I am not arguing that it should. Instead I am arguing against pretending that it should. 3

The important aspect of operating within organizations and systems is that by its very nature it incorporates a predetermined limitation of success. As long as the mission operates under the constraints dictated by the organization's structure, policies, regulations and management philosophies, it will only obtain a finite predetermined level of success. Harari understood that a headquarters' controlled operation automatically hindered his ability to achieve all the objectives implied in the directive set forth by Golda Meir.

The Israeli Prime Minister directed the Mossad to conduct specific covert operations to achieve politically derived strategic objectives. Harari needed to establish a secret compartmentalized operation that was streamlined and efficient. Attempting to work within the official headquarters process would have undoubtedly exposed the mission and/ or possibly slowed it to a nonfunctional level. Outside the official control of the Mossad, Avner's team conducted successful operations without compromise for approximately two years.

Bureaucratic processes are rigid and restrict decentralized authority and the ability to work at a continued fast and fluid pace. Government agencies must live within regulations which do not allow interpretation or flexibility for unique circumstances. Bellman related that organizations are sharply defined and do not allow flexibility. Philip K. Howard, The Death of Common Sense (1995), further demonstrates how this is magnified in government agencies:

Government acts like some extraterrestrial power, not an institution that exists to serve us....It almost never deals with real life problems in a way that reflects an understanding of the situation....Our regulatory system has become an instruction manual. It tells us and the bureaucrats exactly what to do and how to do it. Detailed rule after detailed rule addresses every eventuality, or at least every situation lawmakers and bureaucrats can think of. Is it a coincidence that almost every encounter with government is an exercise in frustration?...In the decades since World War II, we have constructed a system of regulatory law that basically outlaws common sense. Modern law, in an effort to be self-executing, has shut out our humanity....The motives were logical enough: Specific legal mandates would keep government in close check and provide crisp guidelines for private citizens. But it doesn't work. Human activity can't be regulated without judgment by humans....Government cannot accomplish anything when multiple procedures are required for almost every decision....Process is a defensive device; the more procedures, the less government can do....Which is more important: the process or the result? 4

Howard's observations are not unique, but they highlight why Avner's team was so successful. Harari removed the team from the endless regulations and restrictions which the headquarters' process would have imposed. The different agendas of all the bureaucratic elements directing, conducting, and supporting the mission would impose limiting factors relevant to the flow and efficiency of the operation. All of these different elements must adhere to rigid rules and regulations mandated by federal legislation.

While each element attempts to meet all their required procedures, the operational time line is proportionately delayed. Each layer of bureaucracy slows the development of the operation and subsequently limits decentralized authority at the tactical level. For example, the finance branch may require a written request and justification for the use of funds. This element must then identify the proper funding mechanism and acquire authorization to release the funds through their supervisory elements. The request is transferred up and down a chain of command in each element; for every deviation from the original request, amendments for justification must be instituted. The efficiency of the operation is automatically limited by the bureaucratic process. The political authorities create a dilemma, in that they impose factors which cannot possibly be met by adhering to established bureaucratic process. In many cases the process limits the degree of success of a time sensitive operation.

The case studies presented earlier demonstrate the limiting factors inherent in each approach. The Lillehammer affair profiled the elements of a typical headquarters operation. It encapsulates the deficiencies of a sensitive operation controlled through an inefficient bureaucratic process.

The objectives of the mission were sound and in theory the Mossad had the institutional capabilities to conduct the operation with a reasonable expectation of success. The breakdown was in the system itself.

The Mossad incorporated all the internal assets to successfully accomplish the Lillehammer mission. However, the bureaucratic system was not inherently capable of assembling and preparing those assets for a complex mission in a timely manner. The Lillehammer operation required a cohesive team which was well trained in special operations in order to succeed within the specified time parameters. Even the best special operations unit might have failed due to the pace in which the operation was moving, and the lack of rehearsals, geographical knowledge, and positive target identification. Political leaders set political objectives and time restraints which were tactically unreasonable. At best, the mission had high risk "blowback" potential.

The Mossad main headquarters' element orchestrated and controlled the mission. Intelligence obtained through reliable sources placed Salameh in Lillehammer, Norway. Salameh was a primary "hard" target and the Mossad was eager to act on the intelligence. Harari attempted to assemble experienced field officers capable of conducting a sensitive, high risk operation. However, he selected officers in an ad hoc fashion, ostensibly to work together as a cohesive team. In addition, the support team tasked to conduct surveillance, acquire safe houses, and obtain vehicles, was composed of recruited assets. Generally, assets do not operate at the same level of competence and loyalty as staff officers. To this point the operational concepts are sound; however, the introduction of an unrealistic tactical timetable began a domino effect of fatal shortcuts. The team never worked as a coordinated unit prior to this operation, yet they attempted to implement the mission without rehearsals. The ad hoc unit relied on blind faith that all the team members were competent and disciplined in operational trade craft, tactics, and security.

The extremely tight time constraints required dissemination of cables to the field, containing explicit instructions for individual responsibilities, tasks, and escape procedures. Once information began flowing to the field, compartmentalized access of the operation was sacrificed in exchange for time. The operation was moving at a pace in which operational security broke down at almost every level. In their haste to set the mission in motion, team members provided evidence trails of their movements.

This evidence chain enabled police investigators to piece the entire operational network together. Three officers still had compromising material in their possession at the time of their arrest leading the police to other team members. Complacency and lack of good operation trade craft procedures played a big part in the failure, but the primary failure rested in expecting successful results from an operation which was not feasible within the system's constraints. The pace of the mission was beyond the capabilities of the organization. The bureaucratic process was unable to provide the essential elements required to complete the mission successfully in the time allowed. The unit did not have the time to memorize their instructions and closely coordinate or rehearse their actions.

The primary hit team never coordinated with the surveillance team to establish positive identification of Salameh. The results were disastrous. Considering Mossad intelligence, the support teams deployed where they expected to encounter Salameh. The support assets assumed that the individual they had under surveillance was in fact Salameh and continued to operate on that assumption. The movements of the assumed Salameh did not appear to fit the scenario; his stops at the municipal swimming pool, his association with the pregnant female, and the stop at the movie theater. The support team never reported or discussed any of the listed key indicators with the assassination team as particularly unusual for a hard target like Salameh. Still to this point, the operation could possibly have succeeded. It was the responsibility of the assassination team to positively identify their target before taking action.

As the operation unfolded, the primary action element violated the first rule issued to Avner and his team by Harari a year earlier. The Mossad's first rule of engagement in assassination operations provided that officers must obtain absolute identification of the target prior to engagement.

Considering that the mistakes made by the officers involved in the Lillehammer operation were so fundamental in nature, an argument may be made that the officers' either did not possess the requisite skills to conduct such a sensitive mission successfully, or their basic training was inadequate. However, the failure is more attributable to attempting to conduct an operation beyond the capabilities of the political bureaucracy. In the team's rush to meet the political objective of moving against Salameh, they sacrificed routine tactical practices for speed. Apparently Harari and Zamir felt the risk of rushing the operation was acceptable if it provided the Israeli cabinet a successful operation against the PLO which the politicians could positively exploit. The political leadership would be pleased that the Mossad was making progress in their campaign against the PLO and the media could report that the PLO had suffered another serious blow. The Mossad was under extreme pressure from the Israeli cabinet to provide evidence that they were actively pursuing the PLO and making significant progress. Only the few in Committee-X were aware of the full extent of the Mossad's operations against the PLO. The remaining Israeli cabinet members were not briefed on Avner's team and did not understand who was responsible for the killing of so many terrorist leaders, or why the Mossad did not have more reportable information regarding those incidents. 5 The cabinet wanted to see more Israeli influence and reporting. Harari and Zamir probably believed that a successful Mossad operation against Salameh would mollify the cabinet members. In *Vengeance*, George Jonas reported that Harari told Avner, he was under extreme pressure to take "official" action and he was having a great deal of difficulty explaining why the Mossad had not identified the organization moving through Europe killing terrorist leaders. This was one of the primary reasons the IDF conducted the large scale raid into Beirut.

The officers in Lillehammer had more than adequate training and skills; however, the organization forced them to abandon proven trade craft procedures to accomplish the assassination of Salameh under unreasonable tactical conditions. Harari allowed political pressure to dictate the pace of the operation beyond what he knew was reasonably necessary for success within the bureaucracy. This is the primary reason Avner's team was designed outside the political realm of the Mossad. Avner's team would not institute shortcuts bowing to political influences which might jeopardize the success of the mission. Quality operations demand quality people involved and quality planning from the outset. The Mossad team members understood that they would operate in a covert capacity until the successful completion of the mission or the team was no longer able to operate intact due to injuries or deaths. They were to remain a cohesive unit. The unit learned and understood each others' skill, abilities, and limitations, planning and operating accordingly.

TRADE CRAFT, COVER, AND TRAILS OF EVIDENCE

The importance of timely accurate intelligence has never been more critical. As the information highway roars forward nations strive to maintain a strategic, operational, and tactical advantage. Technical intelligence collection has phenomenal capabilities in achieving certain objectives. Imagery, targeting, weapons, and surveillance technologies continue to expand. However, the most difficult operations have always involved human collection (HUMINT). HUMINT involves the development and recruitment of individuals with access to sensitive information which is unattainable through open sources. These recruited assets also play an integral role in the planning of covert operations.

Instituting effective secure covert operations with recruited "agents" or offensive operations through trained operations officers are also extremely difficult tasks. Operating in this modern computerized world makes it almost impossible to operate without creating a "trail" of evidence. The most basic elements of covert operational trade craft address the effective use of cover and trails of evidence. The concepts of developing, maintaining and utilizing cover are essential in effectively deploying covert action teams. Covers may be improvised impulsively to fulfill a quick need, or developed for a long term duration with full headquarters' support. The more complex covers might include the use of proprietary or commercial companies, diplomatic status, or private tourism. Organized crime and terrorist organizations are very proficient in developing very sophisticated "legitimate" business fronts from which to operate. With this in mind, operational planners must understand that the paper trail and legend that follow the moves of the operations officers must support and further establish the bona fides of the officers. Appropriate covers must enhance the probabilities of a successful operation, not hinder it or expose it as a ruse. This concept develops the depth of cover necessary for a reasonable expectation of success. This is the inherent flaw of intelligence agencies operating complex, sensitive operations within a slow moving, rigid bureaucracy.

Effective covert operations demand a flexible capability. Field officers must have the decentralized authority to initiate actions as circumstances dictate to enhance their access and credibility to achieve the end objectives. This is not to say that headquarters' elements should provide carte blanche to operations officers. However, supervisors should understand that the rigidity of the bureaucratic process should not hinder and restrict the officers' ability to succeed. Time is of the essence in high risk operations, and opportunities are won and lost in very short time spans. Field operations cannot afford the luxury of decision by committee.

Politics and The Nature of War

A very serious problem with covert action involves the political factor. As the noted philosopher Karl von Clausewitz related, war is the continuation of policy by other means. As in war, political leaders utilize covert operations to achieve politically driven objectives. The Israeli 'command authority' directed the Mossad to conduct covert operations in much the same way the United States, National Command Authority (NCA) directs its military forces to war to achieve its political objectives.

The inherent concepts are similar in each case. Once the NCA issues its directive, it should not manage the detailed tactical phases of the operation. The NCA generally delegates the strategic, operational, and tactical means to accomplish their directive to the military. In the war on terrorism, the NCA has directed its national resources to counter those individuals or organizations which may target the United States, and prosecute those who have committed acts of violence against U.S. citizens. This is a tall order which demands attention at all levels of the political infrastructure. Political leaders are pressured by the public to demonstrate some success in their endeavors and are watched carefully by the press. Senior officials are very sensitive to the press, and in many circumstances, attempt to modify operations to make them more palatable should sensitive operations become exposed. The initial strategic objectives become muddled in the layers of bureaucracy and competing agendas.

In an effort to accommodate the shifting political environment, sound tactical practices are oftentimes sacrificed. The Israeli Lillehammer incident, and the U.S. Task Force Ranger incident in Somalia, exemplify how quickly operations fail when tactics and sound operational planning was sacrificed for speed to accommodate a politically driven agenda. Politicians and analysts should not dictate and micromanage the tactical aspects of covert operations. However, it is reasonable to fully brief the required political chain of command on the risk potential and probability of success. The action exists to accomplish a political objective in the first place. Based on the merits of these briefings, the political leaders may accept or reject the proposal. However, due to their lack of expertise in tactical operations, politicians should refrain from actually managing field tactics of the mission.

The sensitivity and compartmentalization of an operation is also a very important issue. The methodology of the operation should be consistent with the sensitivity of the mission and the final objective. If a team is designed to be covert yet must be disclosed to endless oversight committees, legal review, interagency courtesy and personnel divisions for administrative concerns, the team becomes vulnerable to exposure in the early stages. In some time sensitive instances, the bureaucratic process defeats the mission before the planning is complete.

Meeting the Objectives

The primary question in the analysis of the two case studies addresses the issue of whether or not the methodologies of the different covert operations succeeded in meeting the final objectives set forth by Golda Meir and Committee-X. The operational objectives must be separated from the political strategy. The political strategy, among a myriad of objectives, was to strike at the heart of the terrorists. Golda Meir wanted to send the message that Israel would not let terrorist acts against Israeli citizens go unanswered or unpunished. There would be a price to pay for any attack on Israeli citizens anywhere in the world. The directive to the Mossad, inherent in the political strategy, was to develop top secret covert operations to track and assassinate the PLO terrorist leaders responsible, either directly or indirectly, for the massacre at Munich. They were to do this while providing a deniability factor for the Israeli government. It was Harari's mission to devise the mechanism to accomplish that task.

To keep the mission compartmentalized, Harari decided to create a team outside the reach of the bureaucracy. This would ensure the secrecy of the mission as well as allowing the team unhampered movement and full decentralized operational control. In the context of tactical and operational objectives, Avner's team achieved enormous success. His team deployed with only a list of eleven primary targets for assassination and two principal rules of engagement. Five of the eleven were effectively tracked and assassinated through Avner's unit's developed network of intelligence and weapons sources. Three additional terrorists were killed in a combined Mossad-IDF commando effort, fully supported through the team's established underground network, Le Group. Ziad Muchassi, was targeted by Avner's team after they learned through Le Group, that Muchassi was the replacement for Abad al-Chir, previously killed by Avner's team. Avner's team made the unilateral decision to assassinate Muchassi since the opportunity presented itself.

Avner's team met all the requirements of their directive to assassinate PLO terrorists while screening any evidence of Israeli government involvement. During the course of their mission, the team also killed four Arab security men employed by the Black September Organization, and one KGB officer supporting BSO activities. In terms of the mission, these individuals could also be considered combatants. They were elements of a security force incorporated in a terrorist organization tasked with the protection of their leaders. These individuals had full knowledge of their association and the risks involved.

Avner's team never compromised the Israeli government's association through exposure to the authorities or arrest. In the context of operational objectives, Avner's team was an unqualified success. The success is directly attributable to the operational design and methodology of the team itself. Five extremely talented officers were selected to work as an independent cohesive unit. They melded their operational trade craft experience in the preparation and implementation of each action without political interference. The effect of streamlining the operation outside the bureaucratic process allowed the team total flexibility. The simplicity of the concept was its genius. Unlike the Lillehammer affair, Avner's team developed, refined, and implemented the actions on a tactically appropriate timetable. If the plan was not feasible at the first opportune time, it was not forced to meet a political agenda.

Instituting a team such as Avner's incorporated a degree of risk, both for the team and the Mossad. Intelligence agencies are very sensitive to losing control of operations. If information of the team, as designed, had leaked, it may have been construed as a rogue team. Although the press did attribute the assassinations to a Mossad covert action team, it was always assumed the team was under the direct control and supervision of the Israeli government. It wasn't until 1984, and the publication of George Jonas' book Vengeance, that the concept of an independent team was exposed.

The mission did result in a number of unforeseen problems. The two year duration placed an enormous stress on the individual team members. The unit became emotionally involved, and paranoid about sharing their intelligence sources with Harari. Although they were dedicated to accomplishing their mission, they began to feel a detachment and sense of disloyalty from the Mossad. When the first of two team members was killed, the team decided to move on their own and conduct an assassination outside the parameters of the PLO terrorists selected by the Mossad. They targeted and assassinated the female freelance assassin responsible for the killing of their colleague. Although sympathetic, the Mossad recognized the emotional decision made by the team and the total disregard of their orders. The problem is not that the woman was an innocent, for she very well may have been contracted by the PLO to target the team.

The major concern was whether or not the Mossad was losing control of the unit. They evaluated the success the team had already achieved in conjunction with their infiltration into the European underground, and apparently determined it was worth the risk of allowing the unit to continue to operate. Technically, the Mossad still had tight control of the unit through their financial resources. The team could only continue to operate as long as the Mossad continued to provide the hard currency required to support the operations. Each assassination was costing approximately $350,000 dollars. The Mossad also controlled the individual accounts of each team member.

Although, for operational purposes, Avner's team was no longer officially associated with the Mossad, they, nevertheless, considered themselves professional Mossad operations officers serving their country. Harari skillfully used their duty as Jewish Israeli citizens as motivation and control.

CHAPTER 5
LESSONS LEARNED

RELEVANCE TO U.S. INTELLIGENCE OPERATIONS

Individuals who have participated in sensitive United States covert operations agreed to comment on the concept of Avner's team and their own experiences, providing their identities remained confidential. Three individuals associated with different agencies and teams provided their input on covert action teams. All three have extensive experience, including close quarter combat which resulted in the deaths of both friendly and enemy personnel. All three acted as the Team Leader of their respective teams' and are identified in alias as Mark, Peter, and Bill.

The teams differed slightly within their respective political infrastructures; however, the critical element of a permanent, cohesive team was consistent. "Permanent" is relative to the assignment's duration in each instance. One example of how an agency designs a special operations group is to utilize three rotating, independent teams, activated for a period of two years; one unit is "on call," one unit is training, and one is pre-paring for deployment. For permanency and cohesiveness, each of the three teams retains its members for the duration of the two year tour.

All three individuals agreed that Avner's team was extremely successful in achieving its operational objectives. Avner's success related directly to the team's combined skills and the permanency of the unit. This, in combination with total freedom of movement and decentralized authority, al-lowed the team to make necessary adjustments quickly. These points were construed as absolutely critical for successful operations.

Careful screening of personnel is also essential in developing competent, cohesive units. The simple fact that officers have similar training does not imply acceptance into an established unit. Uniformly, all three team leaders commented that random substitution of team members is a fatal error. Teams train, rehearse, and deploy together in high risk operations.

They learn each member's strengths and limitations, and develop a "sixth sense" as to how each may react in fluid situations. Their lives depend on each other and they develop a special trust and loyalty within the unit. Unless the bona fides of an officer is clearly substantiated, he will not be fully trusted. Most police or military personnel will not completely rely on a new unit member who is untested or until he/she has proved himself/herself. The teams should incorporate alternate officers who continually train with the unit and may be substituted if a primary member is injured, killed, or indisposed due to personal emergencies.

A common complaint is that politicians and bureaucrats believe that because individuals have common training they may be assembled and deployed on an ad-hoc basis, which is theoretically more economical. Designing a covert action team based primarily on political or economic platforms is a formula for disaster. The Lillehammer incident is a classic demonstration of what can go wrong very quickly.

Mission duration is also a very sensitive element and re-quires close monitoring of the psychological stress on the individual team members. In Mark's team, members worked in a covert capacity ranging from 30 days to nineteen months. The nineteen months was an exceptional case and was monitored very carefully. 1 Peter's team was designed to serve a single purpose, in that each case required extensive surveil-lance culminating with a final operation.

At the completion of an operation, the team would then begin a new, similar mission. Peter's team worked together for approximately three years. 2 Bill's team was a special operations team which responded on short notice to crisis situations. Individuals could work into the team and rotate out throughout the existence of the unit. Integration into the unit involved a very methodical process which insured continuity. 3 Peter's team was finally disassembled due to political pressure. The team achieved significant success, however there were specific outside pressures which the political leadership found possibly detrimental to their careers. It is important to note that none of the three were involved in illegal operations or assassinations.

When the teams were allowed to conduct their operations utilizing good trade craft and tactical techniques, success was almost assured. Of course, there is always an element of risk in every covert operation which extends from mild to high. The goal in extremely high risk operations is to optimize the teams' talents and not to restrict the success ratio by managing the teams' efforts through lawyers and politicians. There is no question that the team serves at the pleasure of the civilian leaders and that the mission is developed to serve political objectives. The disconnect occurs when the leadership attempts to manage the tactical aspects of the operation to ensure peripheral political objectives such as media exploitation and or reelection. The team should consider the operation in relation to the po-litical restrictions imposed and the tactical means necessary to successfully complete it. The success-risk ratio is evaluated, then forwarded back to the higher headquarters for approval or disapproval. This would be ideal in a perfect world.

The problem is that this process is in direct conflict with political realities. At each level in the chain of command is an independent cell with its own goals and objectives. Pressure to succeed, to adhere to every policy and regulation, to be promoted, to fully support higher headquarters, and never say no to a request, are realities. As Bellman pointed out, it is this organization of dysfunctional cells which limits the success of any endeavor attempted through a bureaucracy. The larger the bureaucracy, the less efficient the process becomes.

The trick is to recognize the deficiencies in the system and develop the means to operate at a more efficient level. A former military officer and West Point graduate commented, "...in war, the bureaucracy which makes the fewest mistakes at any particular critical time, emerges as the victor." 4 It is undisputed that gross miscalculations, confused maneuvers, poor command decisions, and misguided political decisions are inherent in every conflict. This is simply the nature of a political, bureaucratic process. The military officer was not simply cynical, he recognized the inherent dynamics of 'systems.' As Bellman related, the answer lies in the ability to recognize the realities and develop methods which work in concert with human nature and not force those methods into mechanically defined boxes on a line chart.

Harari obviously understood the dynamics of the Mossad's political infrastructure. He realized that he would never be able to launch a team like Avner's within the existing structure. It would be impossible to create a highly efficient team capable of multiple operations across Europe, moving from one country to another, on short notice. The paperwork itself would probably have killed the concept. Each move would require new approved orders, advances of funds, travel coordination, notification of regional Stations, weapons moved through slow covert logistical requisitions, and endless justification of accountings.

These mechanisms are necessary to function; however, to fulfill the approval and justification requirements at every level for a sensitive, continuous mission was unacceptable. The mission would also never remain covert with a paper trail of gigantic proportions. Harari's mission was compartmentalized to only the few associated with Committee-X; it was necessary to create a plausible deniability screen for both the public and the Israeli Cabinet.

The Lillehammer incident is indicative of everything which could go wrong in an operation. Not all Mossad headquarters operations ended in disaster; they are, overall, a very proficient and highly respected intelligence service. In the past, it was their ability to carefully develop operations within their system which made them so formidable. The Mossad was small and their operations critical to the country's security. They could not afford to make irreparable mistakes. However, the service grew and evolved into a larger more complex bureaucratic entity and now suffers the inefficiency associated with that growth.

Executive Order 12,333

Although similarities may be drawn between U.S. and Israeli operations, it is important to note that the U.S. operates under much more stringent legal guidelines. The use of assassination is not a legal option in U.S. directed counterterrorist operations. The guidelines on assassination are somewhat complex in the United States, and every president since Ge-rald Ford has attempted to address the issue through the enactment of executive orders. According to Neil C. Livingston, The Cult of Counterterrorism, !989, "there are no statutory prohibitions against assassination, and the United States clearly possesses the capability to carry out so-called 'wet' operations." 5 However, President Gerald Ford felt it necessary to address the issue and subsequently enacted Executive Order No. 11,905 which banned "political assassinations." President Carter expanded the concept under Executive Order No. 12,036. In this order, President Carter removed the word "political," and added the phrase, "no per-son employed by or acting on behalf of the United States Government shall engage in, or conspire to engage in, assassi-nation." 6 President Reagan signed Executive Order No. 12,333, which maintained the same language as President Carter's E.O. 12,036. 7 To date, President Clinton has not en-acted a new executive order and E.O. 12,333 remains in effect.

The United States clearly does not promote the use of assassination in its counterterrorist programs. However, the issue has become somewhat muddled in terms of how E.O. 12,333 applies to military operations. On December 9, 1984, in a speech at the Waldorf-Astoria Hotel in New York, Secretary of State, George P. Shultz, stated that the United States should be prepared to conduct "retaliatory operations" 8 against terrorists. Shultz was echoing President Reagan's sentiments that "swift and effective retribution could be expected" against those terrorists who harm Americans.

After a failed coup attempt in Panama in 1989, DCI Wil-liam Webster addressed the limitations of E.O. 12,333 in an interview with the New York Times. Webster "called upon Congress to give the CIA 'greater latitude' to support coups." 9 Webster specifically addressed the limitations and the confused interpretation of E.O. 12,333. Webster stated, "if you want us to deal with the likes of Noriega, then the law should be changed to allow the CIA to do so." 10 "He told the New York Times that the Congress and President needed to address the ambiguities in the executive order. 'When you have deliberate blurring, it puts a terrible, and I think unacceptable pressure on the people who have to do the work.'" 11

The author recognizes the inherent differences between Israeli and U.S. political realities. Israel, surrounded by hostile borders, must take extraordinary precautions to protect itself. The U.S. does not find itself in the same geopolitical spectrum as Israel. What may be an unacceptable response in a certain situation can, and does, become not only acceptable but morally right, under other circumstances?

NOTES

CHAPTER 1

1George Jonas, author of Vengeance (1984) and investigative journalist, telephone interview by author, January 18, 1995.

2Jonas, interview. Jonas commented that after approximately six
months of discussions with Avner, he concluded that the events described
to him were true. Avner's recall of small details was "excellent." Avner's
recall in combination with Jonas' personal research convinced him that
Avner's account was authentic. Jonas related that he attempted to verify
events through outside sources and establish the likelihood of those
events.

3Avner, former Mossad Operations Officer and primary source to
George Jonas, telephone interview by author, Janu-ary 27, 1995. Source
(Avner) related that due to contractual and confidentiality agreements,
an interview relating to his alleged association with the Mossad would
not be possible. However, he commented that the book, Vengeance, by
George Jonas, describes the details of the Mossad operations subsequent
to the Munich incident, and he could not elaborate beyond what is in
the book. The source (Avner) contacted by the author, further declined
to, confirm or deny, (due to the binding agreements) that he was indeed
Avner. Published open source materials have identified the source as
Avner, but the author chose not to identify the publications or the name
of the individual identified. The source commented that the Israeli Government has officially acknowledged the existence of the independent
assassination teams tasked to target PLO terrorist leaders following the
Munich massacre. Suffice it to say that the fact that the source is restricted

through contractual and confidentiality agreements tends to substantiate the source's identity.

CHAPTER 2

1George Jonas, Vengeance (New York: Simon and Schuster, 1984) 1

2Jonas, 2

3Jonas, 3

4Jonas, 3

5Jonas, 4

6Jonas, 4

7Frank Bolz, Jr., Kenneth J. Dudonis, and David P. Schulz, The Counter-Terrorism Handbook (New York: El-sevier Science Publishing Co., Inc., 1990) 53

8Bolz, 56

9Dan Raviv and Yossi Melman, Every Spy a Prince (Boston: Houghton Mifflin Co., 1990) 184

10Bolz, 56

11Jonas, 6

12Lester Sobel, ed., Facts on File Yearbook (New York: Facts on File Inc., 1973) 695

13Sobel, 695

14Facts on File, 694 (London Times reported on September 6, 1972)

15Raviv, 185

CHAPTER 3

1Facts on file, 695

2Raviv, 186

3Raviv, 186

4Jonas, 350. Jonas relates that according to his sources, the "Wrath of God" name was not officially associated with Av-ner's team.

5Victor Ostrovsky and Claire Hoy, By Way of Decep-tion (New York: St. Martin's Press, 1990) 117-118

6Stewart Steven, The Spymasters of Israel (New York: Bal-lantine Books, 1980)341-349. Steven depicts the events of the Lillehammer operation in detail. There are, however, discrepancies between Steven's biographical sketches of the team members with more recent publications. As described in the bibliography essay and text, it is doubtful that the Mossad had the resources to deploy eight to ten wholly independent teams to conduct assassinations. Within six weeks of the Munich massacre, the Mossad had already accomplished its first successful assassination of Wael Zwaiter; within 12 months, seven successful operations had been completed. This equates to a completed operation approximately every six weeks. This constitutes an incredible recruiting and logistical accomplishment if the Mossad utilized completely independent teams for each operation. It would also indicate an incredible intelli-gence coup if the Mossad was actually capable of tracking and targeting all their targets concurrently.

7Steven, 347

8Steven, 349

9Steven, 346-349

10Jonas, 11

11Jonas, 81

12Jonas, 96

13Jonas, 90

14Jonas, 117

15Jonas, 141-148

16Jonas, 147

17Jonas, 175-254 Jonas provides detailed accounts of Avner's operations against these four targets in his book, Vengeance.

18Jonas, 178-194

19Jonas, 268-280

20Jonas, interview. Jonas commented that he discussed the incidents surrounding the free-lance assassin at length with Avner. Avner maintains that he does not know who targeted his team or contracted the assassin. Avner was adamant that Le Group had not betrayed the team by providing informa-tion about his team to other hostile groups. Avner was not naive, he simply believed that if Papa was going to betray them, he certainly had sufficient prior opportunities. Avner was severely reprimanded for targeting the female assassin and acting outside his established mission parameters. His control officer, Ephraim, was extremely upset.

21Jonas, 294-298

22Jonas, 298

CHAPTER 4

1Ostrovsky, 117-119

2Geoffrey M. Bellman, The Consultant's Calling (San Francisco: Jossey-Bass Inc, Publishers, 1990) 68-70

3Bellman, 71

4Philip K. Howard, The Death of Common Sense (New York: Random House, Inc., 1994) 104, 105

5Jonas, 178

CHAPTER 5

1A source, special operations officer in a federal government agency, who wishes to remain anonymous, conversations with author, January - March 1995.

2A source, special operations officer associated with a major metropolitan police department, who wishes to remain anonymous, conversations with author, January - March 1995.

3A source, special operations officer in a federal government agency, who wishes to remain anonymous, conversations with author, January - March 1995.

4A source, special operations officer in a federal government agency, also a free-lance writer who contributed to international publications, deceased, killed in combat, conversations with author, 1988.

5Neil C. Livingstone, The Cult of Counterterror-ism (Lexington: Lexington Books, 1989) 392

6Livingstone, 392

7Livingstone, 392

8John P. Wolf, Antiterrorist Initiatives (New York: Ple-num Press, 1989) 18

9Mark Perry, Eclipse (New York: William Morrow and Company, Inc., 1992) 290

10Perry, 290

11Perry,291

GLOSSARY

ADVANCE: A support surveillance team which moves a pre-determined distance in front of a target to signal his arrival to a predesignated area; or the reconaissance of an area prior to an operation.

ALIAS: False name and background for cover purposes.

ANTITERRORISM: Passive and defensive measures; activi-ties such as education, foreign liaison training, surveillance, and countersurveillance, designed to deter terrorist activities.

ASSET: Individual recruited by intelligence agency case offi-cers who provides information on sensitive or protected foriegn intelligence, military, political, or economic issues.

BLACK SEPTEMBER
ORGANIZATION: BSO, name utililized from approximately 1971 - 1974, by the Fatah, the military force of the PLO.

CABLE: Messages sent through secure communications chan-nels.

COLLATERAL DAMAGE: Severe injury or death of inno-cents as a result of an operation.

COMMITTEE-X: Special top secret committee within the Is-raeli Cabinet addressing retaliation methods against the PLO for the killing of 11 Israeli citizens at Munich; chaired by Golda Meir and Moshe Dayan.

COVER: Ficticious background devised to support officers in the conduct of covert operations.

COVERT OPERATIONS: Clandestine activities conducted in foreign countries generally conducted by the military or an intelligence agency.

COUNTERTERRORISM: Active measures; operations which incorporate the direct intervention of terrorists groups or the targeting and assassination of terrorist personnel.

EVIDENCE TRAIL: Any evidence establishing the move-ments of officers involved in operations; travel records, passports, hotels, phone records, etc.

FATAH: The military arm of the PLO.

FEDAYEEN: Term used by Islamic terrorists to describe themselves. (term used and explained by George Jonas, in his book, Vengeance.

HUMINT: Acronymn for human intelligence collection.

KIDON: Specially trained elite assassination unit within the Mossad Metsada.

METSADA: Secret organization in the Mossad which operates com-batants.

MOSSAD: Israeli intelligence service.

OFFICIAL COVER: Diplomatic cover utilized by intelligence officers stationed at overseas embassies.

REHEARSAL: Practice walkthrough of an operation prior to the actual event.

SAFE HOUSE: Location used as an operational safe haven that has been acquired through individuals or organizations several levels removed from the officers involved in the opera-tion. The location is generally acquired through legitimate businesses and means, camo-flauging the actual purpose of the complex.

SAYERET: Elite trained reconnaissance forces drawn from the ranks of the Israeli Special Forces.

SIGNAL: Discrete action by one member of a team sending a predeter-mined message to another.

STAFF OFFICER: A fully vetted staff employee of an intelli-gence organization.

SWEEP: Carefully examining a scene for any compromising material or physical evidence which may identify officers in-volved in an opera-tion.

TARGET: Term used to identify the subject of an action.

TRADECRAFT: Special clandestine techniques utilized in covert operations.

BIBLIOGRAPHY

Conducting research on intelligence activities through open sources inherently leaves certain information open to speculation. Even in the best of circumstances, access to classified information does not ensure the absolute confirmation of certain events. Sensitive covert operations are designed to protect the agency and personnel involved with layers of plausible deniability. Sources and methods are protected so that even those with access to the files are unable to verify the names of the individuals involved.

George Jonas, author of Vengeance, published in 1984, provided the primary source of information regarding "Avner's" unit, discussed in depth in this paper. George Jonas is convinced that Avner's account of his mission as the team leader of the Mossad's European independent covert action team is authentic. After discussing Avner's accounts with Jonas, cross referencing the reported assassinations with open source mate-rial, and comparing Avner's account with known trade craft techniques, the author is also convinced that Avner's story is legitimate. Jonas' book addresses specific discrepancies between Avner's account and books published previously. The author also found discrepancies in the identification of personnel and tradecraft techniques in research material, both prior to and subsequent to Jonas' book. The author has attempted to clarify those discrepancies.

Stewart Steven, author of The Spymasters of Israel, published in 1980, speculated that the Mossad recruited independent contractors or foreign assets to fill the teams. An independent contractor is a self-employed individual, hired to conduct specialized duties. Requirements for contractors range from computer specialists to special weapons experts. In this light, Steven stipulated that the Mossad covert team members were independent contractors, not full time Mossad staff officers. Theoretically, contractors were recruited from outside agencies to work as assassins under Mossad control. These persons would undergo preliminary specialized training and subsequently be deployed to the field for the mission. The team members would receive direction, instruction, and sup-port through a Mossad case officer. He further speculated that each operation was conducted by different teams, staffed by different operatives, in each case. His conclusions are based primarily on the widely publicized failed mission in Lille-hammer. He also speculated that the teams had a free hand in their operations, and were used for one mission only, then dis-assembled.

This theory seems unreasonable in that the logistical and security problems would have been enormous. If the Mossad had only 11 terrorists on their primary target list, it would require at least 55 individually recruited contractors to fill the primary "hit" teams. Each team would also require support from regional Stations and recruited assets. Each regional op-eration would also require a minimum of ten support assets to reinforce the primary hit team. This would expose a great number of sensitive assets to temporary employees. The pri-mary team members require a through vetting, alias documents, and essential trade craft training.

This would infer that the Mossad could easily recruit individuals with covert operational skills combined with tactical commando skills, willing to act as assassins. Committee-X and the top secret directive to assassinate PLO terrorist leaders would also be susceptible to exposure. It is ludicrous to believe the Mossad could control over 150 people traveling across the globe targeting PLO terrorists. Even if the Mossad was capable of recruiting the required individuals, it would mandate over a year of processing and training before they could de-ploy to the field.

Avner's team had deployed and completed their first suc-cessful assas-sination of Wael Zwaiter by October 16, 1972, only six weeks after the Munich incident. Victor Ostrovsky, a former Mossad officer, explained in his book, By Way of De-ception (1990) that the Mossad incorpo-rated a special unit to conduct kidnappings and assassinations. This was identified as the Metsada; however, it consisted of only 36 com-mandos di-vided into three teams of twelve, of which only one was operational at any given time.

This still would not account for the number of individuals needed to fill 11 separate, independent teams. In addition, Avner's explanation of duties with the Mossad provided that his prior assignment was with a skymarshal team, not the Metsada or kidon.

Steven's speculations in Spymasters of Israel have been dis-puted in later publications as more reliable information became available. Steven's supposition is contradictory to David B. Tinnin's conclu-sions detailed in an earlier publica-tion, The Hit Team, published in 1976. Steven maintains that Tinnin's premise of a specially trained team moving through the Middle-East and Europe assassinating Arab terrorists was "totally incorrect." Although Steven was able to collect infor-mation on the Lillehammer incident through public sources, information regarding additional teams had not yet surfaced with any supporting evidence.

A separate team was, in fact, traveling through Europe as an indepen-dent entity, targeting terrorists. In addition, the supposition that the hit team consisted of independent con-tractors is also erroneous.

Dan Raviv, co-author of Every Spy a Prince, published in 1990, identi-fied Abraham Gehmer as a Mossad operations of-ficer, working under official cover as First Secretary of the Israeli Embassy in Paris; Stewart Steven listed him as a Mos-sad Commander. Steven believed Dan Arbel was a Danish born, part time Israeli operative, recruited for the Lilleham-mer mission because of his language ability and geographical knowledge of the area. Although the description of his skills may be accurate, Victor Ostrovsky, co-author of By way of Deception (1990), provided that Arbel continued to have a successful career following his arrest. Arbel became the Mos-sad Chief of Station in Paris, and the Chief of the Mossad Training Academy in the mid-eighties. Ostrovsky wrote that he was in training as a Mossad officer at the academy when Arbel was the Chief.

Dorf, Steinberg, and Gladnikoff were described by Steven as recruited assets. At the time of their arrest in Lillehammer, Yigal Zigal presented official Israeli credentials identifying him as an Israeli Embassy security officer and Dorf had an official Station cable in his possession. It would seem highly unusual for someone other than a staff officer to have access to internal classified cables. Since assets are controlled through staff case officers, allowing a recruited asset access to documents containing sensitive and unique Mossad identifiers, would constitute an incredible breach of security.

Harari, Arbel, and Zigal are clearly Mossad staff officers and it is likely that Dorf and Steinberg are as well. This would indicate that the primary action team in Lillehammer was in-deed composed of full time staff officers, not contractors utilized for one mission only. It is feasible that recruited assets were used to fulfill support roles, such as conducting surveil-lance and obtaining vehicles and safehouses. "Local" assets assimilate more easily into the area and are not readily identi-fied through language deficiencies or physical appearance. The information provided to these support officers is routinely lim-ited and

compartmentalized to avoid exposing an entire operation if individuals
are compromised.

The books, Spymasters of Israel, By Way of Decep-tion, Eclipse, and
Every Spy a Prince, identified Mike Harari as the coordinator of the
Mossad assassination teams. Mr. Jonas, through Avner's account, maintains that the original supposi-tions made in earlier publications that
independent contractors were recruited to fulfill the mission require-
ment is incorrect. Other sources also speculated that teams formed for
this mission were born out of Ariel Sharon's Squad 101. Ac-cording
to Jonas, Squad 101 was conceived in the late 1950's of special trained
commandos to fight the fedayeen in the Gaza Strip and Israeli borders.
The new teams formed by Gen-eral Zamir were different in organization and personnel selection. These teams were indeed filled by
Mossad staff offi-cers. Also, officers recruited into the Mossad routinely
have previous military and commando training.

Made in United States
Troutdale, OR
07/26/2023

11566283R00046